Introduction

Reading comprehension involves numerous thinking skills. The ability to differentiate between fact and opinion is one such skill. A reader who can identify these two types of statements is better able to analyze and assess a t  While distinguishing fact from opinion is one step in reading, it is importan that students go further. They should also be able to sort facts and opinions to help determine the writer's point of view. Exercises 1–18 provide practice in learning to distinguish between statements of fact and opinion. Exercises 19–35 focus on determining point of view. Use pages 8 and 9 after you introduce the skills to give students help in understanding them.

Using This Book

Pages 8–9

After introducing fact and opinion and point of view to students (see pages 6 and 7), duplicate and pass out pages 8 and 9. Use page 8 to help students review what they have learned about identifying fact and opinion. By explaining their thinking, students are using metacognition to analyze how they recognized and utilized these clues. Page 9 helps students review what they have learned about point of view.

Pages 10–27

These pages offer practice in distinguishing **fact** from **opinion**. Students should read the paragraph, then identify the selected sentences in item 1 as fact or opinion. Items 2 and 3 call for students to write another fact or opinion from the paragraph. Tell students that the sentences they write should not be any of those used in item 1.

Pages 28–44

These pages provide exercises in determining **point of view**. Students should read the paragraph, then describe the writer's opinion about the topic. Item 2 requires students to identify a key word in the paragraph. Item 3 calls for students to recognize the writer's point of view, and item 4 asks students to identify another possible viewpoint.

Pages 45–46

After they have completed the practice pages, use these pages to assess students' progress.

Page 47

You may wish to keep a record of students' progress as they complete the practice pages. Sample comments that will help you guide students to improving skills might include:

- reads carelessly
- misunderstands text
- fails to recognize clues
- doesn't apply prior knowledge

Teaching About Fact and Opinion

1. Introduce the concept: Write these statements on the chalkboard.

Our school is in session Monday through Friday.
I think there should be classes on Saturday.

Ask students which statement can be proved. Which statement is what someone believes?

2. Model thinking: After students have correctly recognized that the first statement can be proved and the second statement is what you believe, continue the lesson by thinking aloud.

I know that our school is open Monday through Friday because I teach here. That is something I can prove. The first statement is a fact.

The second statement tells what I think. Most schools are not open for classes on Saturday, but I still think it's a good idea. The words *I think* and *should* are clues that this statement is an opinion.

3. Define the skill: Tell students that a fact can be proved to be true. Sometimes you can see the proof easily; sometimes you can check a fact in a reference book. Facts answer these questions: *Who? What? Where? When? Why? How?*

Remind students that references such as encyclopedias, almanacs, textbooks, biographies, and other nonfiction books all contain facts. So do newspapers, magazines, and Internet sites. (You may wish to caution students that not all information on the Internet is reliable.)

Explain that an **opinion** may or may not be true. An opinion is what someone believes; it is a kind of judgment. There may be many opinions about a subject. Opinions can be based on facts or on feelings. Some opinions contain clue words such as *I believe, I feel, I think, in my judgment, most, best, should, must, better than, worst.*

Caution students that not all opinions have clue words. An opinion can be stated like this:

Saturday classes are a great idea.

Explain that opinions are found in advertisements, feature stories, editorials, and many other types of writing.

SCHOLASTIC

POINT OF VIEW & FACT AND OPINION

by Linda Ward Beech

NEW YORK • TORONTO • LONDON • AUCKLAND • SYDNEY
MEXICO CITY • NEW DELHI • HONG KONG • BUENOS AIRES

Teaching *Resources*

Cover design by Maria Lilja
Interior design by Sydney Wright
Interior illustrations by Mike Gordon

ISBN-13 978-0-439-55413-8
ISBN-10 0-439-55413-6

1 2 3 4 5 6 7 8 9 10   40   14 13 12 11 10 09 08 07 06

Contents

Teaching About Point of View

1. Introduce the concept: Read these three descriptions to students.

> Mel's dog Rags is digging a hole in the neighbor's garden. Stop that, Rags!
>
> Rags is sleeping on Mom's new couch. You're not allowed there, Rags!
>
> Rags is playing fetch with Mel. Good boy!

Ask students to tell how the neighbor, Mom, and Mel might think about Rags.

2. Model thinking: After students have correctly described different points of view about Rags, help them review the process they used by thinking aloud.

> The neighbor is angry at Rags. I would certainly feel that way if a dog dug up my garden.

> Mom may like Rags, but she's worried about her couch. The word *new* gives me a clue about her feelings. Some dogs get hair all over furniture.

> Mel likes to play fetch with his dog.

3. Define the skill: Explain that people express different points of view in their writing. Often, these points of view are based on facts and opinions. In many cases, feelings are involved, too. It is important to try to identify a writer's point of view and then compare it with what you yourself think. Mention that the point of view of an expert, based on knowledge and experience, is usually valuable and worth reading. A viewpoint based on firsthand experience or from an eyewitness often offers new insights into a situation. Considering other points of view doesn't mean you have to agree, but it can help broaden a reader's understanding of a subject. Good readers consult several sources on subjects of interest to them.

What Is a Fact? What Is an Opinion?

When you read a nonfiction passage, you are usually reading facts. However, the passage may also contain opinions. How does a reader sort facts from opinions? A reader might think:

Which statements can be proved?

Which statements reflect what the writer thinks or believes?

When you answer the first question, you identify the **facts**. These are statements that can be proved or observed. When you answer the second question, you determine **opinions**. An opinion is a judgment that reflects a person's beliefs or feelings. It is not necessarily true.

Read the paragraph. Answer the questions.

One of the most wonderful dogs is the Saint Bernard. This large, strong animal has a thick coat and a good sense of direction. In the Alps of Switzerland, Saint Bernards have been used as guides to help travelers through mountain passes. As the dogs pass through thick snow, their deep chests form tracks that people can follow. Saint Bernards are sometimes used to help rescue skiers who get lost on snowy slopes.

What facts are given in this paragraph?

1 Who or what is the paragraph about? _____

2 What traits do these animals have? _____

_____

3 How are these animals helpful to people? _____

What opinion is given?

4 What judgment does the writer make about the subject? _____

_____

5 How could you prove that the facts are true? _____

_____

What Is a Point of View?

When you read a selection, you find both facts and opinions. Many accounts also reflect the writer's point of view or how the writer feels about the subject. A good reader tries to determine what the writer's point of view is. A reader might think:

What opinions are expressed?

What kinds of words are used to describe people, places, and events? Are these words positive? Negative? How do they express the writer's feelings?

Do I agree with this point of view?

What might another point of view be?

When you answer the first question, you recognize that an opinion is being given. The second question helps you look more closely at the point of view of the writer. When you answer the last two questions, you are thinking about how the writer's point of view affects the information given.

Read the paragraph. Answer the questions.

Do you like amusing sights? If so, you should have seen the tree growing from a chimney at Tyler House. This building is a dorm on a college campus in Massachusetts. The tree, a type of aspen, apparently seeded itself with the help of the wind. Aspens grow best in sunny spots, and the chimney offered plenty of sunshine. Unfortunately, the tree's roots were growing into the bricks and mortar, so the enterprising tree had to be removed.

1 What does the writer think is an "amusing sight"? _____

_____

2 Which word tells how the writer feels about the tree?

Ⓐ sunny   Ⓑ enterprising   Ⓒ unsafe

3 Why do you agree or disagree with the writer's point of view? _____

_____

4 What point of view might someone from the local fire department have?

_____

Fact and Opinion

Read the paragraph. Follow the directions.

In Britain, judges and lawyers have traditionally worn wigs and gowns in court. Depending on their role, some also wear lace neck trimmings, sashes, hoods, fur mantles, and buckled shoes. From time to time, this judicial finery has been mocked. After all, it is ridiculous. The curly wigs are made in four shades of off-white, ranging from light gray to beige. The more important the official, the fancier the wig. A senior judge wears a headpiece of curls that reaches to the shoulders. What a silly, fusty, dusty custom!

1 Write *fact* or *opinion* next to each sentence.

In Britain, judges and lawyers have traditionally worn wigs and gowns in court.

_____

From time to time, this judicial finery has been mocked. _____

What a silly, fusty, dusty custom! _____

2 Write another fact from the paragraph. _____

_____

_____

3 Write another opinion from the paragraph. _____

_____

_____

Fact and Opinion

Read the paragraph. Follow the directions.

Isaac Asimov was the finest American author. He was born in Russia in 1920 but came to the United States with his family when he was three. Asimov became a professor of biochemistry and a writer. Most of his books were about science fiction. *Fantastic Voyage* was definitely his best book. Many of Asimov's stories featured robots and, with another writer, he created the Three Laws of Robotics. These govern how robots behave in science fiction.

1 Write *fact* or *opinion* next to each sentence.

Isaac Asimov was the finest American author. _____

Asimov became a professor of biochemistry and a writer. _____

Most of his books were about science fiction. _____

2 Write another fact from the paragraph. _____

_____

_____

3 Write another opinion from the paragraph. _____

_____

_____

EXERCISE
3

Fact and Opinion

Read the paragraph. Follow the directions.

Most surfers find their waves in the ocean, but in Brazil, surfers find them in the Amazon River. Each March and April, when the river waters are highest, strong tides from the Atlantic Ocean push into the Amazon basin. These tides create a giant swell that travels upstream for hundreds of miles at speeds of 20 miles an hour. Brazilians call this endless wave a *pororoca*. Surfing for miles up the river is much more fun than a short ocean ride. All surfers should try this unique challenge.

1 Write *fact* or *opinion* next to each sentence.

Brazilians call this endless wave a *pororoca*. _____

All surfers should try this unique challenge. _____

These tides create a giant swell that travels upstream for hundreds of miles at

speeds of 20 miles an hour. _____

2 Write another fact from the paragraph. _____

_____

_____

3 Write another opinion from the paragraph. _____

_____

_____

Scholastic Teaching Resources   *Point of View & Fact and Opinion*

Fact and Opinion

Read the paragraph. Follow the directions.

How lucky we are when snow begins to fall! Something beautiful is coming our way because the geometry of a snowflake is spectacular. Snowflakes form when water vapor condenses into crystals. Although snowflakes are never identical, they all have a six-pointed symmetry in common. However, weather conditions affect the final shape of a snowflake. These conditions include the temperature and the amount of water vapor in the air. Each snowflake is a work of art.

1 Write *fact* or *opinion* next to each sentence.

How lucky we are when snow begins to fall! _____

Something beautiful is coming our way because the geometry of a snowflake

is spectacular. _____

Although snowflakes are never identical, they all have a six-pointed

symmetry in common. _____

2 Write another fact from the paragraph. _____

_____

_____

3 Write another opinion from the paragraph. _____

_____

_____

Fact and Opinion

Read the paragraph. Follow the directions.

A feature of many modern houses is the Palladian window. This window, with its three panels and curved top, takes its name from the architect Andrea Palladio. He lived in the sixteenth century in Italy. That was an excellent time for talented people. Palladio studied the architecture of the ancient Romans. No one could build like the Romans. During his lifetime, Palladio designed villas, churches, and other public buildings. Visitors to Italy can still see many of these buildings today.

1 Write *fact* or *opinion* next to each sentence.

A feature of many modern houses is the Palladian window. _____

No one could build like the Romans. _____

Visitors to Italy can still see many of these buildings today. _____

2 Write another fact from the paragraph. _____

_____

_____

3 Write another opinion from the paragraph. _____

_____

_____

Fact and Opinion

Read the paragraph. Follow the directions.

The first emperor of China must have been strange.
He spent much of his life planning for his tomb.
It took 700,000 workers 36 years to get it ready. In
the tomb were 6,000 life-size soldiers made from
terra-cotta, a kind of pottery. Each soldier had an
individual face, just like the soldiers in the emperor's
real army. I think this is bizarre. Also in the tomb
were carriages and horses made from bronze. The
tomb was a big secret for thousands of years. Then,
some farmers found it while digging a well in 1974.

1 Write *fact* or *opinion* next to each sentence.

The first emperor of China must have been strange. _____

It took 700,000 workers 36 years to get it ready. _____

Then, some farmers found it while digging a well in 1974. _____

2 Write another fact from the paragraph. _____

_____

_____

3 Write another opinion from the paragraph. _____

_____

_____

Fact and Opinion

Read the paragraph. Follow the directions.

Millions of people in Japan write poetry. That is such a great thing! Everyone should write poems. Everyone should be passionate about poetry. Japan has regular radio and television programs about poetry. It also has more than 2,000 poetry magazines and newsletters. The country's national newspapers carry poetry columns on a daily basis. Books of poetry are best-sellers. I wish they were in other nations. Many Japanese companies hold poetry contests. One company prints the winners on its packages.

> Loving the idea
> Of poetry for people,
> I created poems.

1 Write *fact* or *opinion* next to each sentence.

That is such a great thing! _____

Everyone should write poems. _____

Books of poetry are best-sellers. _____

2 Write another fact from the paragraph. _____

_____

_____

3 Write another opinion from the paragraph. _____

_____

_____

Fact and Opinion

Read the paragraph. Follow the directions.

People have been living with domesticated animals for thousands of years. For example, dogs and people go back about 14,000 years. Believe me, dogs are "man's best friend." Cats have been around for a long time, too. The ancient Egyptians thought of cats as gods. People should remember that because most cats today think of themselves as gods! Both children and adults should have pets. Birds, rabbits, and some types of fish are popular pets. I don't think they're as satisfying as dogs and cats, though.

1 Write *fact* or *opinion* next to each sentence.

Both children and adults should have pets. _____

The ancient Egyptians thought of cats as gods. _____

Believe me, dogs are "man's best friend." _____

2 Write another fact from the paragraph. _____

_____

_____

3 Write another opinion from the paragraph. _____

_____

_____

Fact and Opinion

Read the paragraph. Follow the directions.

Have you ever noticed that the print in comic strips is in capital letters? I find this really annoying. One reason given is that comic strips are reduced when printed in newspapers. When print is reduced, small letters tend to blob up more than big ones. Another reason is that by using letters that are the same height, an artist can fit them in the space more easily. I think that artists probably find using lowercase letters too much of a challenge. Maybe they don't know which words to capitalize!

SMALL LETTERS VARY IN HEIGHT.

1 Write *fact* or *opinion* next to each sentence.

Have you ever noticed that the print in comic strips is in capital letters?

_____

When print is reduced, small letters tend to blob up more than big ones.

_____

Maybe they don't know which words to capitalize! _____

2 Write another fact from the paragraph. _____

_____

_____

3 Write another opinion from the paragraph. _____

_____

_____

Scholastic Teaching Resources   *Point of View & Fact and Opinion*

Fact and Opinion

Read the paragraph. Follow the directions.

In Korea, people mark a child's first birthday with a celebration called *tol*. On this occasion, it is believed that babies pick their future. The child sits at a table covered with different objects. If the child picks a string, it means a long life. Everyone should pick that. If a baby picks money or rice, it indicates a business career. A musical instrument means the child will become an artist. That's a good choice. A special rice-cake soup is served at *tol* celebrations. I think cake and ice cream are better.

1 Write *fact* or *opinion* next to each sentence.

The child sits at a table covered with different objects. _____

Everyone should pick that. _____

A special rice-cake soup is served at *tol* celebrations. _____

2 Write another fact from the paragraph. _____

_____

_____

3 Write another opinion from the paragraph. _____

_____

_____

Fact and Opinion

Read the paragraph. Follow the directions.

You should visit Strawbery Banke in Portsmouth, New Hampshire. This is a settlement that is now an outdoor history museum. Parts of Strawbery Banke were built in the 1600s; others are more recent. Visitors can see how people lived during three centuries in American history. It's really interesting. The guides dress as people did during each period. They act as if they were living during that time. They make barrels, pottery, baked goods, and other things. You'll enjoy this place.

PORTSMOUTH

1 Write *fact* or *opinion* next to each sentence.

You should visit Strawbery Banke in Portsmouth, New Hampshire.

_____

Parts of Strawbery Banke were built in the 1600s; others are more recent.

_____

It's really interesting. _____

2 Write another fact from the paragraph. _____

_____

_____

3 Write another opinion from the paragraph. _____

_____

_____

Fact and Opinion

Read the paragraph. Follow the directions.

A huge mountain system stretches across 1,500 miles of Asia. This mountain range is called the Himalayas. The mountains were formed about 60 million years ago. The world's 10 tallest mountains are all in the Himalayas. That's amazing! Mount Everest, which lies between Tibet and Nepal, is the world's highest mountain. It reaches up for 29,028 feet, too high for even birds to fly. The first climbers to reach the top did so in 1953. They must have been brave. Their names were Sir Edmund Hillary and Tenzing Norgay.

1 Write *fact* or *opinion* next to each sentence.

This mountain range is called the Himalayas. _____

That's amazing! _____

The first climbers to reach the top did so in 1953. _____

2 Write another fact from the paragraph. _____

_____

_____

3 Write another opinion from the paragraph. _____

_____

_____

Fact and Opinion

Read the paragraph. Follow the directions.

Kids who like to get muddy should visit Westland, Michigan. This city hosts an annual celebration called Mud Day in Hines Park. It must be a sloppy mess. The parks department mixes more than 200 tons of soil and 20,000 gallons of water to make mud. That's a lot of mud! There are events such as a Mud Limbo contest, wheelbarrow races, and just plain splashing around. Two participants are crowned Mr. and Miss Mud. When the fun is over, firefighters hose down the dirty kids.

Write *fact* or *opinion* next to each sentence.

1 Kids who like to get muddy should visit Westland, Michigan. _____

It must be a sloppy mess. _____

Two participants are crowned Mr. and Miss Mud. _____

2 Write another fact from the paragraph. _____

_____

_____

3 Write another opinion from the paragraph. _____

_____

_____

Scholastic Teaching Resources   Point of View & Fact and Opinion

Fact and Opinion

Read the paragraph. Follow the directions.

Eartha is the world's largest moving globe. If you see it, you'll feel a sense of wonder. Eartha is more than 41 feet in diameter and weighs about 5,600 pounds. It rotates just like planet Earth. It was developed from computer technology and is made from one of the largest mapping databases in the world. To visit Eartha, you have to go to Yarmouth, Maine. The globe is housed in a three-story glass building there. It's very impressive.

1 Write *fact* or *opinion* next to each sentence.

If you see it, you'll feel a sense of wonder. _____

It rotates just like planet Earth. _____

To visit Eartha, you have to go to Yarmouth, Maine. _____

2 Write another fact from the paragraph. _____

_____

_____

3 Write another opinion from the paragraph. _____

_____

_____

Fact and Opinion

Read the paragraph. Follow the directions.

Many living things have internal clocks. These are daily patterns known as circadian rhythms. One of the most common is the pattern of sleep that humans follow. Certain flowers have patterns, too. These flowers open and close their petals on specific schedules. For example, dandelions open at nine in the morning. People should get rid of dandelions because they're weeds. A morning glory opens at 10 A.M., and a water lily at 11. My favorite flower is the California poppy. Its petals open at 1 P.M.

1 Write *fact* or *opinion* next to each sentence.

Many living things have internal clocks. _____

My favorite flower is the California poppy. _____

For example, dandelions open at nine in the morning. _____

2 Write another fact from the paragraph. _____

_____

_____

3 Write another opinion from the paragraph. _____

_____

_____

Scholastic Teaching Resources   *Point of View & Fact and Opinion*

Fact and Opinion

Read the paragraph. Follow the directions.

A good way to spend free time is by playing games. During the Civil War (1861–1865), both Union and Confederate soldiers had time between battles. So the troops amused themselves in different ways. The Union soldiers played a popular board game called "The Checkered Game of Life." It was such a terrific game! Whoever invented it must have been very clever. A version of this game is still around today. It is now called "The Game of Life." Have you ever played it?

1 Write *fact* or *opinion* next to each sentence.

The Union soldiers played a popular board game called "The Checkered Game of Life." _____

A good way to spend free time is by playing games. _____

It was such a terrific game! _____

2 Write another fact from the paragraph. _____

_____

_____

3 Write another opinion from the paragraph. _____

_____

_____

EXERCISE
17

Fact and Opinion

Read the paragraph. Follow the directions.

A large granite head rises out of Thunderhead Mountain in South Dakota. The head is magnificent. It is part of a sculpture called the Crazy Horse Memorial, which is being carved from the mountain. Crazy Horse was a Sioux warrior who defeated Lieutenant Colonel George Armstrong Custer at the Battle of Little Bighorn in 1877. The memorial was begun in 1948 by Korzak Ziolkowski. It's taken much too long to complete. When finished, however, it will be 563 feet tall and 641 feet long.

1 Write *fact* or *opinion* next to each sentence.

A large granite head rises out of Thunderhead Mountain in South Dakota.

_____

The memorial was begun in 1948 by Korzak Ziolkowski. _____

It's taken much too long to complete. _____

2 Write another fact from the paragraph. _____

_____

_____

3 Write another opinion from the paragraph. _____

_____

_____

Scholastic Teaching Resources   *Point of View & Fact and Opinion*

Name _____   Date _____

Fact and Opinion

Read the paragraph. Follow the directions.

You should thank the Navajos. During World War II, 350 of them worked as code talkers. They sent messages in the Navajo language for the American military. Both sides used codes during the war, but most codes can eventually be broken. You have to be brilliant to break a code. However, little of the Navajo language had ever been written down, it was hard to learn, and it was very different from other languages. So although many radio messages were intercepted, the enemy couldn't break the Navajo code.

1 Write *fact* or *opinion* next to each sentence.

You should thank the Navajos. _____

They sent messages in the Navajo language for the American military.

_____

Both sides used codes during the war, but most codes can eventually

be broken. _____

2 Write another fact from the paragraph. _____

_____

_____

3 Write another opinion from the paragraph. _____

_____

_____

EXERCISE

19

Point of View

Read the paragraph. Answer the questions.

Gerardus Mercator, born in 1512, is known for a kind of map. His map—called a Mercator Projection—has caused unfair distortions of the world. For example, the Northern Hemisphere on a Mercator map dominates the world. Greenland appears as big as Africa. Yet Greenland is much smaller than the African continent. North America appears much larger than South America. No doubt, the overblown proportions of places on the map have made people there think of themselves as more important, too.

1 What is the writer's opinion of the distortions on Mercator's map?

_____

2 Which word in the passage is a clue to how the writer feels about the map's proportions?

Ⓐ smaller   Ⓑ larger   Ⓒ overblown

3 Which phrase best reflects the writer's point of view?

Ⓐ Admires the mapmaker Gerardus Mercator

Ⓑ Blames Mercator for distorted worldviews

Ⓒ Supports the domination of the Northern Hemisphere

4 What point of view might someone living in Greenland have? _____

_____

_____

Scholastic Teaching Resources   Point of View & Fact and Opinion

Point of View

Read the paragraph. Answer the questions.

France has long been known as a country where people are devoted to their dogs. At some Paris hotels, this is no exception. They offer many services just for the canine set. For example, there are trained dog groomers, charming dog toiletries, and even custom-made beds for pampered pets. These wonderful hotels also provide round-the-clock room service for dogs, with a choice of healthy meals. Of course, dogs are welcome in the hotel restaurants, too. They can't get in without their owners, though!

1 What is the writer's opinion of the treatment of dogs in France?

_____

2 Which word in the passage is a clue to how the writer feels about the hotel services?

(A) wonderful   (B) healthy   (C) exception

3 Which phrase best reflects the writer's point of view?

(A) Approving of the dog treatment

(B) Upset with the hotels

(C) Outraged about so much attention being given to dogs

4 What point of view might someone who can't make ends meet have? _____

_____

_____

Point of View

Read the paragraph. Answer the questions.

Marjory Stoneman Douglas was the heroine of the Everglades, a unique environment in Florida. Many animals make their home in this wetland region. Nevertheless, for years the Everglades were being drained off for buildings and roads. The water was polluted. So Douglas wrote a book, *The Everglades: River of Grass*. In it she explained why the Everglades were important and should be protected. In 1969, Douglas started an organization called Friends of the Everglades. The Friends kept an airport from being built there!

1 What is the writer's opinion of Marjory Stoneman Douglas? _____

_____

2 Which word in the passage is a clue to how the writer feels about the Everglades?

(A) polluted   (B) home   (C) unique

3 Which phrase best reflects the writer's point of view?

(A) Annoyed by the work of Douglas

(B) Uninterested in the fate of the Everglades

(C) Impressed by the efforts of Douglas

4 What point of view might a builder have about Marjory Stoneman Douglas?

_____

_____

Point of View

Read the paragraph. Answer the questions.

Scientists say that nature is really amazing. Recently, some scientists were studying a strange sponge found deep in the Pacific Ocean. They insisted that filaments on the sponge were much like optical fibers used in telecommunication systems. Their somewhat dubious plan was to study the sponge with the hope of duplicating its features for future uses. What those uses are, the scientists haven't said. Stay tuned!

---

1 What is the writer's opinion of nature? _____

_____

2 Which word in the passage is a clue to how the writer feels about the scientists' plan of study?

Ⓐ dubious   Ⓑ amazing   Ⓒ hope

3 Which phrase best reflects the writer's point of view?

Ⓐ Awed by scientists and nature

Ⓑ Skeptical about the sponge study

Ⓒ Excited about the sponge project

4 What point of view might a scientist in the study have? _____

_____

_____

EXERCISE

23

Point of View

Read the paragraph. Answer the questions.

Poor spellers shouldn't try to sell things through online ads. Suppose you want to sell a camera on eBay, but your ad says "Camra for Sale." Buyers looking for cameras aren't likely to find *your* ad. However, some clever buyers are on the lookout for misspelled ads written by careless sellers. When they find one, they offer a low bid. Since no one else is bidding for the item, the seller often lets the item go for a low price. Often, the smart buyers then turn around and sell the item for more—through an ad that's spelled correctly!

1 What is the writer's opinion of buyers who look for misspellings? _____

_____

2 Which word in the passage is a clue to how the writer feels about sellers who misspell?

  Ⓐ clever   Ⓑ careless   Ⓒ smart

3 Which phrase best reflects the writer's point of view?

  Ⓐ Sympathetic to spelling problems

  Ⓑ Disappointed by poor spelling

  Ⓒ Impatient with poor spellers

4 What point of view might a poor speller have? _____

_____

_____

Scholastic Teaching Resources   *Point of View & Fact and Opinion*

Point of View

Read the paragraph. Answer the questions.

Fans love racehorses that win. Curiously, a horse in Japan became a favorite for losing. The horse, named Haruurara, ran more than 100 races—and lost them all. Then a news story featured this four-legged loser. Suddenly, Haruurara had lots of devoted fans. The Japanese began to think of her as a lucky charm. People thought if they lost with Haruurara, they wouldn't lose other things such as their jobs or homes. So backing a racing loser became popular. Some would say it was a no-win situation!

1 What is the writer's opinion of Haruurara? _____

_____

2 Which word in the passage is a clue to how the writer feels about Haruurara's fame?

　Ⓐ devoted　　　Ⓑ curiously　　　Ⓒ popular

3 Which phrase best reflects the writer's point of view?

　Ⓐ Amused by the unusual story

　Ⓑ Angered by the horse's losses

　Ⓒ Shocked by the idea of lucky charms

4 What point of view might the owner of the horse have? _____

_____

_____

Point of View

Read the paragraph. Answer the questions.

I was awakened from a deep sleep the other morning by the awful noise of a car alarm. It was the kind that goes off in an unpleasant, repetitive way every few minutes. Finally, someone came and drove the offending vehicle away. The next morning, I awoke to the same annoying sound. When I looked out the window, there was no car. All I saw was a mockingbird on my fence. And sure enough, that remarkable bird was imitating a car alarm. I have to admit it was quite a performance.

1 What is the writer's opinion of car alarms? _____

_____

2 Which word in the passage is a clue to how the writer feels about the mockingbird?

Ⓐ offending   Ⓑ repetitive   Ⓒ remarkable

3 Which phrase best reflects the writer's point of view?

Ⓐ Joyful enthusiasm

Ⓑ Reluctant admiration

Ⓒ Bored

4 What point of view might the neighborhood cat have? _____

_____

_____

Scholastic Teaching Resources   Point of View & Fact and Opinion

EXERCISE

26

Point of View

Read the paragraph. Answer the questions.

Watch out for wet dogs. They shake water all over and often smell funny. Many people attribute this smell to a dog's fur. However, a strong odor from a wet dog is more likely to be caused by a skin problem, not wet fur. Some dogs such as cocker spaniels and terriers get rashes and skin irritations that result in body odor. Water can make the odor more noticeable. According to dog experts, the best way to prevent smelly dogs is by grooming them regularly.

1 What is the writer's opinion of wet dogs? _____

_____

2 Which word in the passage is a clue to how the writer feels about the odor of

wet dogs?

Ⓐ funny   Ⓑ grooming   Ⓒ attribute

3 Which phrase best reflects the writer's point of view?

Ⓐ Worried about wet dogs

Ⓑ Interested in helping dog owners

Ⓒ Delighted by dog smells

4 What point of view might a cat lover have? _____

_____

_____

Point of View

Read the paragraph. Answer the questions.

Do you like fruitcake? Strangely enough, some people do like it! They actually think this heavy, sticky cake is good enough to eat. Most people agree that fruitcake is an English holiday tradition. Most people also think that it's better to give a fruitcake than to receive one. In fact, many people who receive fruitcakes as gifts quickly give them away to someone else. One famous writer even went so far as to say that "nobody in the history of the United States has ever bought a fruitcake for himself."

1 What is the writer's opinion of people who like fruitcake? _____

_____

2 Which word in the passage is a clue to how the writer feels about fruitcake?

Ⓐ good   Ⓑ strangely   Ⓒ tradition

3 Which phrase best reflects the writer's point of view?

Ⓐ Admiring of fruitcake

Ⓑ Worried about fruitcake eaters

Ⓒ Mocking of fruitcake

4 What point of view might a fruitcake baker have? _____

_____

EXERCISE
28

Point of View

Read the paragraph. Answer the questions.

Do dolphins and people have a special relationship? Over the centuries, many civilizations have told stories of bonds between people and these incredible creatures. In an ancient Greek story, the god Dionysus changes some pirates into dolphins. An Australian myth tells about a hero named Gowonda who turned into a helpful dolphin. In a tale from Peru, a pink dolphin sometimes becomes a human. Even today, people report stories of dolphins helping swimmers or guiding ships through dangerous seas.

1 What is the writer's opinion of dolphins? _____

_____

2 Which word in the passage is a clue to how the writer feels about dolphins?

Ⓐ incredible   Ⓑ pink   Ⓒ dangerous

3 Which phrase best reflects the writer's point of view?

Ⓐ Unimpressed by dolphins and their relationship with people

Ⓑ Admiration of dolphins and their relationship with people

Ⓒ Angry about dolphins and their relationship with people

4 What point of view might a sailor have about dolphins? _____

_____

_____

EXERCISE

29

Point of View

Read the paragraph. Answer the questions.

Tigers are the biggest members of the cat family.
These magnificent cats are solitary animals and
need a large territory in which to hunt. They mark
their territory with urine so that other tigers are
warned away. Tigers track their prey in silence and
then pounce for the kill. A tiger can eat 40 pounds
of meat in one meal. Unfortunately, tiger habitats have been destroyed in many
parts of Asia, their homeland. Scientists think there may be only 3,000 to 6,000
tigers left in the wild. These mighty animals are close to extinction.

1 What is the writer's opinion of the appearance of tigers? _____

_____

2 Which word in the passage is a clue to how the writer feels about the strength

of tigers?

Ⓐ prey   Ⓑ solitary   Ⓒ mighty

3 Which phrase best reflects the writer's point of view?

Ⓐ Regretful about the loss of tigers

Ⓑ Joyful about the habitat of tigers

Ⓒ Curious about the fate of tigers

4 What point of view might a person living near the tigers' habitat have about tigers?

_____

_____

Scholastic Teaching Resources   Point of View & Fact and Opinion

Name _____ Date _____

Point of View

Read the paragraph. Answer the questions.

Almost all bridges have them. I'm speaking of signs that say "Caution: Bridge Freezes Before Road." Many people wonder why it is that bridges freeze first. The answer is simple. A bridge is exposed to air both from above and below. When the temperature drops, heat accumulated in the bridge is released. A road, on the other hand, is only exposed to the environment from above. Heat retained in the ground actually provides insulation for roads so they take longer to freeze. So the important bridge signs help keep drivers safe.

1 What is the writer's opinion of the signs on bridges? _____

_____

2 Which word in the passage is a clue to how the writer feels about the signs?

Ⓐ important   Ⓑ simple   Ⓒ exposed

3 Which phrase best reflects the writer's point of view?

Ⓐ Appreciative of the signs

Ⓑ Mystified by the signs

Ⓒ Leery of the signs

4 What point of view might a car driver have about the bridge signs? _____

_____

_____

Point of View

Read the paragraph. Answer the questions.

Niagara Falls is known for people who like to, well, go over the edge. The first mindless daredevil was Annie Edson Taylor in 1901. Bobby Leach went over in 1911, breaking not only his jaw but both kneecaps as well. Some of the next attempts didn't fare well at all. While Roger Woodward survived his trip over the falls in 1960, he never meant to go in the first place. He had a boating accident. Two people in one barrel made it over safely in 1989. Two more in a plastic capsule succeeded in 1995. So, who's next?

1 What is the writer's opinion of people who go over Niagara Falls? _____

_____

2 Which word in the passage is a clue to how the writer feels about Annie Edson Taylor?

   Ⓐ mindless   Ⓑ survived   Ⓒ safely

3 Which phrase best reflects the writer's point of view?

   Ⓐ Disapproving of these actions

   Ⓑ Sorry about these actions

   Ⓒ Startled by these actions

4 What point of view might an extreme sports enthusiast have about going over the falls?

_____

_____

EXERCISE

32

Point of View

Read the paragraph. Answer the questions.

Diwali is a happy and delightful holiday that is celebrated by Hindus around the world. Diwali is sometimes called the Festival of Lights. Lamps brighten streets, line building rooftops, and shine from windows. Hindus believe that Lakshmi, the goddess of wealth, uses the lamps to guide her way as she comes to bless homes. Diwali also symbolizes the victory of good over evil. For Hindus, this holiday is the beginning of the New Year. People wear new clothes and eat special foods on this very festive day.

1 What is the writer's opinion of Diwali? _____

_____

2 Which word in the passage is a clue to how the writer feels about Diwali?

Ⓐ evil   Ⓑ festive   Ⓒ shine

3 Which phrase best reflects the writer's point of view?

Ⓐ Fearful about this holiday

Ⓑ Enthusiastic about this holiday

Ⓒ Indifferent to this holiday

4 What point of view might an electrician have about this holiday? _____

_____

_____

Point of View

Read the paragraph. Answer the questions.

Streets were a mess in 1923. Not only that, they were downright dangerous. Cars drove through intersections without stopping. So did horse-drawn carriages and bicyclists. Lots of accidents happened, and many people were injured. Then Garrett Morgan invented the electric traffic signal. What a difference! Now drivers knew when to proceed or stop. Morgan's ingenious invention, one of many he made in his lifetime, was the beginning of the traffic light system we use today. This inventor should be thanked!

1 What is the writer's opinion of the traffic light? _____

_____

2 Which word in the passage is a clue to how the writer feels about this invention?

Ⓐ dangerous   Ⓑ electric   Ⓒ ingenious

3 Which phrase best reflects the writer's point of view?

Ⓐ Weary of Garrett Morgan

Ⓑ Admiring of Garrett Morgan

Ⓒ Uncertain about Garrett Morgan

4 What point of view might a car manufacturer have about this invention?

_____

_____

Scholastic Teaching Resources   Point of View & Fact and Opinion

Point of View

Read the paragraph. Answer the questions.

Samuel Goldwyn was a powerful figure in
Hollywood during the twentieth century. He
made many famous movies. One of these was
Wuthering Heights, based on the book by Emily
Brontë. However, Goldwyn often bungled his
English and usually referred to the movie as
"Withering Heights." Other amusing things he
said were "Include me out" and "I'll give you
a definite maybe." Goldwyn also said, "I don't think anyone should write his
autobiography until after he's dead." Well, he *was* in the entertainment business.

1 What is the writer's opinion of Samuel Goldwyn? _____

_____

2 Which word in the passage is a clue to how the writer feels about Goldwyn's quotes?

Ⓐ amusing   Ⓑ powerful   Ⓒ famous

3 Which phrase best reflects the writer's point of view?

Ⓐ Annoyed by Goldwyn's statements

Ⓑ Uncomfortable with Goldwyn's statements

Ⓒ Entertained by Goldwyn's statements

4 What point of view might a competitor of Goldwyn's have about his statements?

_____

_____

EXERCISE
35

Point of View

Read the paragraph. Answer the questions.

How did wealthy people spend leisure time in the late 1800s? One fascinating pastime was to exchange afternoon visits. At each house, a visitor would leave an elegant calling card. These printed cards included the  person's name, much like a business card of today. The cards would be placed on a tray and taken by a servant to the lady of the house. The hostess would then decide to accept the visit, decline the visit, or postpone the visit. After World War I, telephones and cars led to the end of this quaint social custom.

1 What is the writer's opinion of the use of calling cards? _____

_____

2 Which word in the passage is a clue to how the writer feels about the use of calling cards?

Ⓐ wealthy   Ⓑ quaint   Ⓒ printed

3 Which phrase best reflects the writer's point of view?

Ⓐ Shocked by the custom

Ⓑ Distressed by the custom

Ⓒ Intrigued by the custom

4 What point of view might a hostess of the late nineteenth century have about calling cards? _____

_____

Scholastic Teaching Resources   Point of View & Fact and Opinion

Fact and Opinion

Read the paragraph. Follow the directions.

Vegetables and fruits of the future may differ from those you eat today. Scientists in China have been sending seeds into space. The seeds are exposed to different extraterrestrial conditions such as cosmic radiation or zero gravity. These trips to space alter the DNA of the seeds. The seeds are then planted back on Earth. The results are disturbing. Some examples are cucumbers the length of baseball bats and monster eggplants. They must taste terrible. These veggies aren't for sale to the public yet. They're probably not safe!

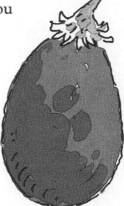

1 Identify three statements of fact in the paragraph.

- _____

- _____

- _____

2 How would you express the writer's opinion about space veggies? _____

_____

_____

3 Identify two statements in the paragraph that support your answer to item 2.

- _____

- _____

Point of View

Read the paragraph. Answer the questions.

You're probably aware of extreme sports such as dangling from bungee cords over cliffs. But have you heard about extreme ironing? The first Extreme Ironing World Championships took place in Germany in 2002. Top contestants included ironists with names such as Starch and Steam. They pressed clothes while scaling a wall, hanging from tree branches, and balancing on ironing boards. No kidding! Since then ironists have attacked wrinkled clothing all over the world. They've ironed while riding bicycles, scuba diving, and even climbing Mount Everest. Wow! Starch manufacturers must be thrilled.

1 How would you express the writer's point of view about extreme ironing?

_____

_____

2 List three words or phrases that helped you determine the point of view.

- _____

- _____

- _____

Name _____ Date _____

Student Record

Date	Exercise #	Number Correct	Comments

Scholastic Teaching Resources   *Point of View & Fact and Opinion*

Answers

page 8:
1. Saint Bernard dogs
2. Possible: They have a good sense of direction.
3. Possible: They can rescue lost skiers.
4. Possible: The writer thinks Saint Bernards are the most wonderful dogs.
5. Answers will vary.

page 9:
1. The writer finds amusing a tree growing from a chimney.
2. B
3. Answers will vary.
4. Possible: A tree near a chimney is a fire hazard.

page 10
1. fact, fact, opinion
2. Possible: A senior judge wears a headpiece of curls that reaches to the shoulders.
3. After all, it is ridiculous.

page 11:
1. opinion, fact, fact
2. Possible: He was born in Russia in 1920 but came to the United States with his family when he was three.
3. *Fantastic Voyage* was definitely his best book.

page 12:
1. fact, opinion, fact
2. Possible: Most surfers find their waves in the ocean, but in Brazil, surfers find them in the Amazon River.
3. Surfing for miles up the river is much more fun than a short ocean ride.

page 13:
1. opinion, opinion, fact
2. Possible: Snowflakes form when water vapor condenses into crystals.
3. Each snowflake is a work of art.

page 14:
1. fact, opinion, fact
2. Possible: This window, with its three panels and curved top, takes its name from the architect Andrea Palladio.
3. That was an excellent time for talented people.

page 15:
1. opinion, fact, fact
2. Possible: He spent much of his life planning for his tomb.
3. I think this is bizarre.

page 16:
1. opinion, opinion, fact
2. Possible: Japan has regular radio and television programs about poetry.
3. Everyone should be passionate about poetry.

page 17:
1. opinion, fact, opinion
2. Possible: Cats have been around for a long time, too.
3. Possible: People should remember that because most cats today think of themselves as gods.

page 18:
1. fact, fact, opinion
2. Possible: One reason given is that comic strips are reduced when printed in newspapers.
3. Possible: I find this really annoying.

page 19:
1. fact, opinion, fact
2. Possible: In Korea, people mark a child's first birthday with a celebration called *tol*.
3. Possible: That's a good choice.

page 20:
1. opinion, fact, opinion
2. Possible: This is a settlement that is now an outdoor history museum.
3. You'll enjoy this place.

page 21:
1. fact, opinion, fact
2. Possible: A huge mountain system stretches across 1,500 miles of Asia.
3. They must have been brave.

page 22:
1. opinion, opinion, fact
2. Possible: This city hosts an annual celebration called Mud Day in Hines Park.
3. That's a lot of mud!

page 23:
1. opinion, fact, fact
2. It's very impressive.
3. Possible: Eartha is more than 41 feet in diameter and weighs about 5,600 pounds.

page 24:
1. fact, opinion, fact
2. Possible: These are daily patterns known as circadian rhythms.
3. People should get rid of dandelions because they're weeds.

page 25:
1. fact, opinion, opinion
2. Possible: During the Civil War (1861–1865), both Union and Confederate soldiers had time between battles.
3. Whoever invented it must have been very clever.

page 26:
1. fact, fact, opinion
2. Possible: It is part of a sculpture called the Crazy Horse Memorial, which is being carved from the mountain.
3. The head is magnificent.

page 27:
1. opinion, fact, fact
2. Possible: During World War II, 350 of them worked as code talkers.
3. You have to be brilliant to break a code.

page 28:
1. Possible: The writer is concerned about them because of their inaccuracies.
2. C
3. B
4. Possible: People might be pleased because it makes Greenland seem more important.

page 29:
1. Possible: The writer thinks the treatment is great.
2. A
3. A
4. Possible: That person might think that it is unfair to spend so much money on dogs when people need help.

page 30:
1. Possible: The writer admires the work of Douglas.
2. C
3. C
4. Possible: A builder might think parts of the Everglades should be developed.

page 31:
1. Possible: The writer is not convinced that scientists know what they are doing.
2. A
3. B

page 32:
1. Possible: The writer thinks they are smart.
2. B
3. C
4. Possible: A poor speller might be upset or annoyed by these facts.

page 33:
1. Possible: The writer is surprised that a losing horse is so popular.
2. B
3. A
4. Possible: The owner might be pleased because of the horse's popularity.

page 34:
1. Possible: The writer thinks they make an awful noise.
2. C
3. B
4. Possible: The cat might be confused by a bird that sounds like a car.

page 35:
1. Possible: The writer is not fond of the smell of wet dogs.
2. A
3. B
4. Possible: A cat lover might be uninterested in dog problems.

page 36:
1. Possible: The writer thinks they are curious and strange.
2. B
3. C
4. Possible: A baker might adore fruitcake and be offended by the writer's opinion.

page 37:
1. Possible: The writer seems to admire dolphins.
2. A
3. B
4. Possible: A sailor may think dolphins are special.

page 38:
1. Possible: The writer thinks they are magnificent.
2. C
3. A
4. Possible: A person living near the tigers' habitat might be concerned about being attacked.

page 39:
1. Possible: The writer thinks they are useful.
2. A
3. A

4. Possible: Scientists might feel there are good uses for the sponge.

4. Possible: A driver might wonder why bridges freeze first.

page 40:
1. Possible: The writer thinks these people are foolish.
2. A
3. A
4. Possible: An extreme sports enthusiast might approve of people's attempts.

page 41:
1. Possible: The writer favors Diwali.
2. B
3. B
4. Answers will vary. Possible: An electrician might like Diwali because it calls for so many lights.

page 42:
1. Possible: The writer approves of the traffic light.
2. C
3. B
4. Possible: A car manufacturer might be in favor because it promotes order and safety for drivers.

page 43:
1. Possible: The writer seems to admire Goldwyn.
2. A
3. C
4. Possible: A competitor might not find them amusing.

page 44:
1. Possible: The writer finds the custom quaint.
2. B
3. C
4. Possible: A hostess might find them useful.

page 45:
1. Possible: Scientists in China have been sending seeds into space. The seeds are exposed to different extraterrestrial conditions such as radiation or zero gravity. The seeds are then planted back on Earth.
2. Possible: The writer is upset about space veggies.
3. Possible: The results are disturbing. They're probably not safe!

page 46:
1. Possible: The writer is amused but somewhat tongue-in-cheek about extreme ironing.
2. Possible: No kidding! Wow! Starch manufacturers must be thrilled.

Scholastic Teaching Resources   Point of View & Fact and Opinion